the science of CATASTROPHE

HUMAN-MADE DISASTERS

Steve Parker & David West

Crabtree Publishing Company

www.crabtreebooks.com

Crabtree Publishing Company

www.crabtreebooks.com

Created and produced by:
David West Children's Books

Project development and concept:
David West Children's Books

Authors: Steve Parker and David West

Editor: Adrianna Morganelli

Proofreader: Crystal Sikkens

Designer: David West

Illustrator: David West

Project coordinator: Kathy Middleton

Production and print coordinator: Katherine Berti

Prepress technician: Katherine Berti

Library and Archives Canada Cataloguing in Publication

Parker, Steve, 1952-
    Human-made disasters / Steve Parker and David West.

(The science of catastrophe)
Includes index.
Issued also in electronic formats.
ISBN 978-0-7787-7575-1 (bound).--ISBN 978-0-7787-7580-5 (pbk.)

    1. Disasters--Juvenile literature. 2. Nature--Effect of human beings on--Juvenile literature. I. West, David, 1956- II. Title. III. Series: Science of catastrophe

D24.P37 2011   j904'.7   C2011-905013-7

Library of Congress Cataloging-in-Publication Data

Parker, Steve, 1952-
  Human-made disasters / Steve Parker & David West.
    p. cm. -- (The science of catastrophe)
  Includes index.
  ISBN 978-0-7787-7575-1 (reinforced library binding : alk. paper) --
ISBN 978-0-7787-7580-5 (pbk. : alk. paper) -- ISBN 978-1-4271-8858-8
(electronic pdf) -- ISBN 978-1-4271-9761-0 (electronic html.)
  1. Disasters--Juvenile literature. 2. Nature--Effect of human beings on--
Juvenile literature. I. West, David, 1956- II. Title. III. Series.

  GB5019.P37 2012
  904--dc23

                                            2011027739

Crabtree Publishing Company

www.crabtreebooks.com   1-800-387-7650

Printed in the U.S.A./112011/JA20111018

Published in Canada
Crabtree Publishing
616 Welland Ave.
St. Catharines, Ontario
L2M 5V6

Published in the United States
Crabtree Publishing
PMB 59051
350 Fifth Avenue, 59th Floor
New York, New York 10118

Published in the United Kingdom
Crabtree Publishing
Maritime House
Basin Road North, Hove
BN41 1WR

Published in Australia
Crabtree Publishing
3 Charles Street
Coburg North
VIC 3058

Contents

Boiler Explosion

March 18, 1912, seemed like just another day at the railroad yard in San Antonio, Texas. Workers checked and mended locomotives and wagons. One man turned the wrong tap on Locomotive No. 704 and…BOOM!

The Harrisburg & San Antonio Railroad, in Galveston, was suffering from the Great Southwest Strike. Regular workers stayed away from the Southern Pacific Railroad Yard in protest against daily dangers such as runaway wagons, fires, and overheating locomotives.

Strike-breakers were brought from northern and eastern cities. They left one locomotive standing but with its boiler heating. The water level inside ran low and the steam, with nowhere to go, built up to incredible pressure. Without realizing, a worker opened the cold-water tap. Now the steam could escape—with the force of a big bomb. San Antonio was shaken as if by an earthquake. Nearby buildings blew away, and windows smashed for many blocks around. Many workers died instantly. The locomotive's boiler ended up three blocks away. About 35 victims died and another 50 suffered horrific burns and injuries. Rail companies at last realized that they must improve safety.

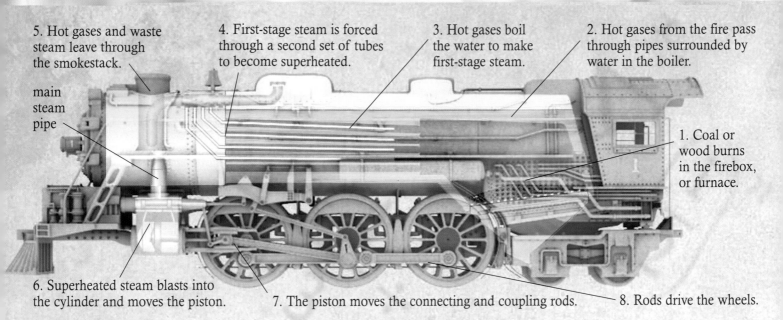

5. Hot gases and waste steam leave through the smokestack.

4. First-stage steam is forced through a second set of tubes to become superheated.

3. Hot gases boil the water to make first-stage steam.

2. Hot gases from the fire pass through pipes surrounded by water in the boiler.

main steam pipe

1. Coal or wood burns in the firebox, or furnace.

6. Superheated steam blasts into the cylinder and moves the piston.

7. The piston moves the connecting and coupling rods.

8. Rods drive the wheels.

THE SCIENCE OF STEAM ENGINES

Fuel, such as coal or wood, burns in the firebox (furnace). The hot smoke and flue gases pass into a cluster of pipes called smoke or boiler tubes inside the large water-filled boiler. The water becomes so hot that it boils into steam. This collects at the front of the boiler and then passes through a second set of superheater tubes to make it even hotter with greater pressure. The superheated steam flows down the main steam pipes into the cylinder, pushing the piston inside to and fro. Sets of rods turn the **reciprocating** motion into the round-and-round motion of the wheels.

In an instant, and almost without warning, the quiet Southern Pacific yard suffered a giant explosion, as if a bomb had detonated. (Artist's depiction)

Just before midnight, in dark, icy seas, Titanic *rams against a mountainous iceberg. (Artist's depiction)*

THE SCIENCE OF FLOATING AND SINKING

An object in water pushes aside, or displaces, some of that water. If the displaced water weighs more than the object, then the object has **buoyancy** and floats. If the displaced water weighs less, it sinks. Big ships have separate watertight compartments, so even if one or two take in water, they still float. *Titanic* would float with four compartments flooded—but the iceberg damaged six.

Ocean Liner Sinking

Perhaps the widest-known ocean tragedy is the sinking of the ocean liner Titanic, after it struck an iceberg on April 14–15, 1912. A century later, arguments continue about what happened, why, and who was to blame.

Even before it sank, RMS *Titanic* was the most famous ship of its day. It was the newest, biggest, and most luxurious ship, with every comfort. It was on its first voyage from Southampton, England, to New York, U.S.A. The 883-foot (269-meter) long ship, weighing 52,000 tons (47,174 metric tons), was carrying 2,200 passengers and crew.

Four days after leaving Southampton, the great ocean liner steamed through the cold waters of the Northwest Atlantic near Grand Banks, Newfoundland. It had already been warned about icebergs in the area by radio messages from nearby ships. But these messages did not pass from the radio room to the ship's bridge (control center). The bridge crew were unaware of the danger.

At 11:40 p.m., a lookout saw an iceberg dead ahead. There was no time to change course. The impact broke and flooded six of *Titanic's* watertight compartments. There were far too few lifeboats for everyone on board, and nearby ships did not respond to the emergency radio signals. Two hours and 40 minutes later, *Titanic* sank in the freezing water. The death toll was 1,500, with 700 survivors picked up two hours later. The disaster led to new laws about enough lifeboats and better radios on ships.

In 1985, the *Titanic* wreck was located 12,450 feet (3,800 meters) down on the sea bed, about 370 miles (600 kilometers) from Newfoundland. It has since been explored several times by deep-sea submersibles.

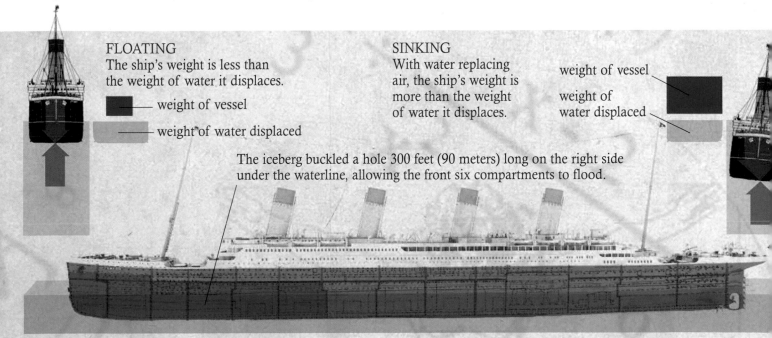

FLOATING
The ship's weight is less than the weight of water it displaces.

weight of vessel

weight of water displaced

SINKING
With water replacing air, the ship's weight is more than the weight of water it displaces.

weight of vessel

weight of water displaced

The iceberg buckled a hole 300 feet (90 meters) long on the right side under the waterline, allowing the front six compartments to flood.

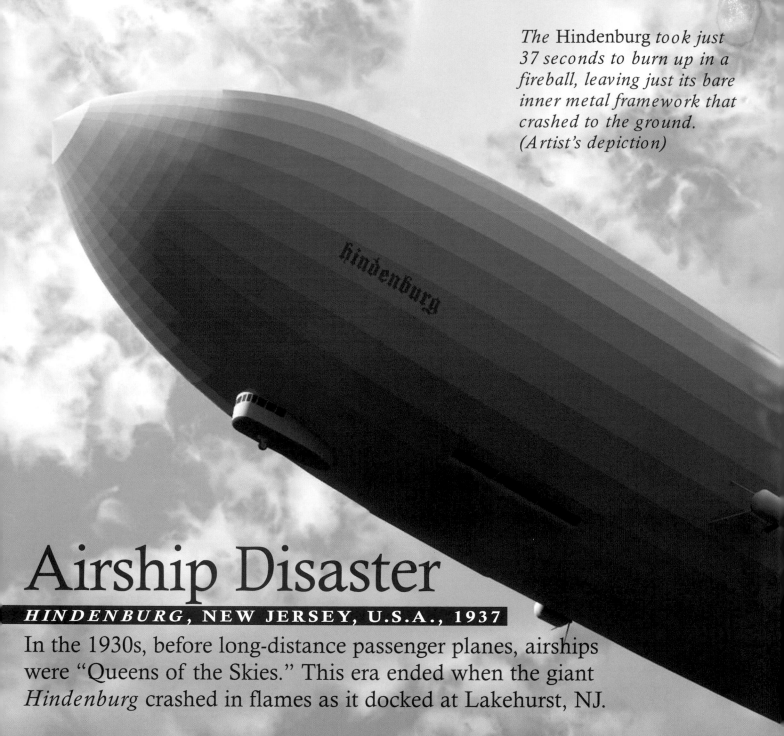

The Hindenburg *took just 37 seconds to burn up in a fireball, leaving just its bare inner metal framework that crashed to the ground. (Artist's depiction)*

Airship Disaster

HINDENBURG, NEW JERSEY, U.S.A., 1937

In the 1930s, before long-distance passenger planes, airships were "Queens of the Skies." This era ended when the giant *Hindenburg* crashed in flames as it docked at Lakehurst, NJ.

In the 1930s, ocean liners took up to a week to journey between North America and Europe. Airships took half the time, with almost equal luxury, and offered fabulous views—if the weather allowed. After a season of successful trips in 1936, the airship *Hindenburg*, built in pre-WWII Nazi-era Germany, approached its mooring tower at Lakehurst Naval Air Station, in New Jersey, U.S.A., at 7:20 p.m. on May 6, 1937. This was the local "airship-port" for the New York area. Suddenly the colossal "gas-bag" of hydrogen caught fire and the craft burst into flames. The cause was believed to be a spark of **static electricity** jumping between the airship and the earth. Of the 97 people on board, 13 passengers and 22 crew died, plus one ground crew member. Public reaction to the horrific scenes meant that airship travel was doomed. Faster, safer passenger planes soon took over.

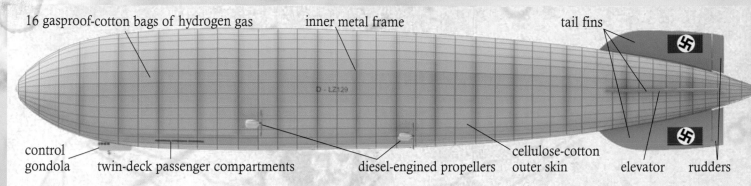

16 gasproof-cotton bags of hydrogen gas   inner metal frame   tail fins

control gondola   twin-deck passenger compartments   diesel-engined propellers   cellulose-cotton outer skin   elevator   rudders

THE SCIENCE OF AIRSHIPS

Airships stay up because they are filled with lighter-than-air gas. In *Hindenburg's* time this was hydrogen, which catches fire easily. (Modern airships, like party balloons, use helium, which does not catch fire.) Propellers gave forward thrust. On the tail fins, upright rudders steered left or right, with horizontal **elevators** to climb or descend. *Hindenburg* was longer than any other aircraft ever, at 804 feet (245 meters)—more than three times the length of a modern Boeing 747 Jumbo Jet. It carried just 72 passengers.

Workers rush to the aid of miners lucky enough to escape after the explosion at Benxihu Colliery. (Artist's depiction)

Mining Tragedy

Mining and quarrying have long, tragic histories of terrible accidents and loss of life. The worst-ever disaster occurred during World War II at Benxihu Colliery coal mine, where at least 1,500 people died.

During the 1930s, Japan took over parts of north and northeast China. The Japanese masters forced local Chinese people to work in terrible conditions of poverty and disease. One of the worst places was Benxihu Colliery (once called Honkeiko Colliery) near the industrial city of Benxi. Coal was needed to fuel furnaces for making iron, steel, and other metals. During the 1940s, conditions for the Chinese miners got worse. They were fenced in, beaten, and almost starved. Safety equipment and precautions were ignored. In the stale air and dim, dusty conditions, many were truly worked to death.

On April 26, 1942, a huge coal-dust and gas explosion ripped through the tunnels. To prevent the fire from spreading to other areas of the site, the Japanese bosses quickly turned off the ventilation fans, closed the air shafts, and sealed the tunnel entrances. Inside, workers died of their burns or slowly suffocated in the smoke. Outside, electric fences kept reporters and relatives away, to keep the size of the accident a secret. The first death toll announced was just 30 to 40. But gradually the full extent of the horror became clear. Eventually the number of dead was estimated at 1,500—but it was probably many more.

THE SCIENCE OF FIREDAMP AND COAL-DUST EXPLOSIONS

Firedamp is a mix of natural vapors that seep from the walls of caves, caverns, and tunnels, especially in coal mines. One vapor is methane, the main burnable gas in natural gas fuels. Coal-dust is tiny particles of coal that float and settle. Because the dust is surrounded by a combination of air and firedamp vapors, it catches fire and burns very fast, like an explosion. In modern mines, filters remove these deadly hazards.

1. Firedamp vapors seep from coal seams.

2. A spark ignites the vapors, which explode.

3. Shock waves from the explosion blow settled coal-dust into the air.

4. Coal-dust burns in a fireball that travels along the tunnel.

Industrial Explosion

TEXAS CITY, TEXAS, U.S.A., 1947

The worst industrial catastrophe in U.S. history happened on April 16, 1947. The seaport of Texas City, just north of Galveston, Texas, was almost flattened by a series of massive explosions that killed over 580 people. It all started with a small fire on board the aging cargo ship SS *Grandcamp*…

Grandcamp was loaded with 3,200 tons (2,903 metric tons) of the dangerous chemical ammonium nitrate from Midwest factories. Railroaded to Texas City in paper sacks, it was bound for Europe, for industrial processes such as making fertilizers and explosives. Around 8 a.m., smoke came from the *Grandcamp*. The cause of this initial fire was never clear. The ship got hotter and the water around steamed. Local firefighters came, with spectators nearby on the dockside. Then BANG!—the chemical exploded in a huge blast. It ripped the ship to pieces and smashed apart hundreds of buildings. Windows blew out in Houston, over 40 miles (65 kilometers) away. More explosions and fires started all around Texas City, in ships, along docks, and in warehouses containing wood, oil, textiles, and other **flammable** materials.

No one knows the final death toll. Many bodies were shredded by the blast or burned away. Estimates were 581 deaths, but there could have been many more. Over 5,000 people were injured and 2,000 made homeless. The aftermath led to many new rules about packing, storing, and transporting dangerous materials.

THE SCIENCE OF CHEMICAL EXPLOSIONS

Ammonium nitrate is one of many chemicals that slowly decomposes, or breaks up, to produce heat and give off vapors. Poor packing lets the effects of heat spread. Any kind of spark from electrical equipment or metal parts knocking can ignite ammonium nitrate. The chemical can even make so much heat itself that it undergoes **spontaneous combustion**.

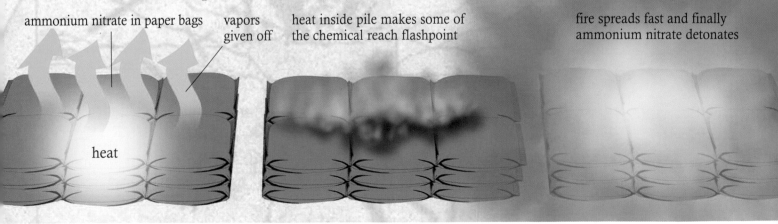

ammonium nitrate in paper bags

vapors given off

heat inside pile makes some of the chemical reach flashpoint

fire spreads fast and finally ammonium nitrate detonates

heat

Grandcamp's *fire worsens before the explosion.* (*Artist's depiction*)

The gaping hole in Banqiao Dam allows water to surge far across the countryside, drowning people, animals, and whole villages and towns. (Artist's depiction)

THE SCIENCE OF DAMS

A dam is a wall or barrier across a river or lake to keep back water. This water fills the area behind, forming a reservoir. The oldest design is the embankment type, where the wall is thickest at the base, to withstand the greatest water pressure deep in the reservoir. In narrow valleys, concrete arch and cupola designs are curved, to cope better with the immense stresses. Many newer dams generate power, known as hydroelectricity, from the energy of the moving water.

Dam Failure

The world's worst dam collapse was just after midnight on August 8, 1975. Extremely heavy rain led to a series of catastrophic failures along the River Ru, centered on the Banqiao Dam near Zhumadian, Henan Province, China.

The Banqiao Dam was one of more than 60 in the area. Of clay embankment design, it was built in the early 1950s to control serious flooding and also create a reservoir for water during dry spells. Soon after completion, and again in the 1960s, cracks appeared. Experts recommended more **sluice gates** but the authorities only patched up the dam.

On August 6–7, extra-powerful typhoon storms dumped more rain on the area in two days, than usually fell in a whole year. Local officials suggested opening some of the dams by targeted bombing from military aircraft. This would cause flooding, but in a slow, controlled manner. However telegram and telephone lines were down and messages went astray. Then the Shimantan Dam upstream gave way, allowing a huge rush of water to Banqiao. The clay wall could not cope and broke. The over-filled, pent-up reservoir poured through the gap and spread in a wave up to 23 feet (seven meters) high and eight miles (13 kilometers) wide, flooding an area 35 miles (55 kilometers) long. Over 30,000 people died in the torrents, and another 150,000-plus from the famine and disease that followed. Five million buildings were swept away, making ten million people homeless.

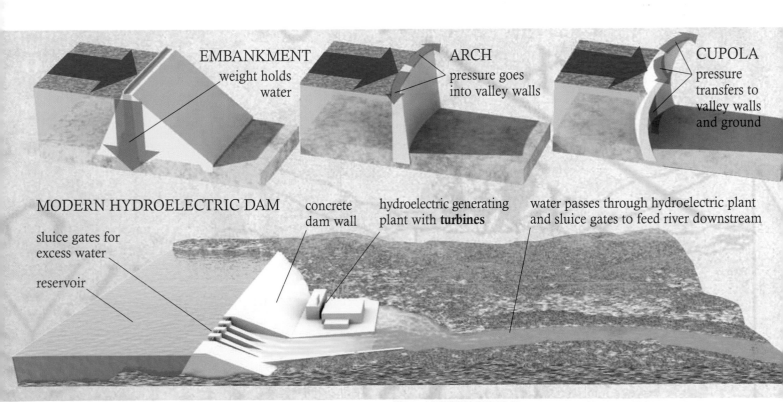

EMBANKMENT
weight holds water

ARCH
pressure goes into valley walls

CUPOLA
pressure transfers to valley walls and ground

MODERN HYDROELECTRIC DAM

concrete dam wall

hydroelectric generating plant with **turbines**

water passes through hydroelectric plant and sluice gates to feed river downstream

sluice gates for excess water

reservoir

Poison Gas Leak

UNION CARBIDE CHEMICAL FACTORY, BHOPAL, INDIA, 1984

One of the most sinister catastrophes is caused by invisible poison gases floating in the air. By the time people feel the effects, their bodies may be harmed beyond repair. This happened in Bhopal City, capital of the central Indian state of Madhya Pradesh, on December 2–3, 1984.

The Bhopal chemical plant made **carbaryl** pesticide to kill insects and other harmful bugs. One of the substances it used was methyl isocyanate, MIC. Even tiny amounts cause coughing, breathing problems, chest pain, skin damage, and severely irritated eyes, nose, and throat. By law, MIC has long been a controlled chemical, needing many safety precautions. The Bhopal factory was run down, with broken pumps, rusty pipes, leaky valves, and dripping taps. Somehow water got in a storage tank of MIC. The chemical reaction caused by the two substances made the tank's emergency valves open to let out the high-pressure gases. A cloud of heavy, poisonous vapors seeped across the city.

People woke coughing and choking, their eyes and noses streaming. As they ran outside into the gases, the effects worsened. The deadly cloud lingered for hours. More than 7,000 people died quickly, and another 10,000 over the following months and years. Over 4,000 survivors had severe permanent injuries. Another half a million suffered some kind of harm. Union Carbide paid almost half a billion dollars for the terrible damage.

THE SCIENCE OF REACTION AND PRESSURE

Chemical stores should be clearly labeled with their contents, the hazards, and action in case of a leak or break. Tanks need emergency valves and safety vents that open automatically if the pressure builds up inside, to prevent an explosion, and also alarms to warn this is happening. At Bhopal, the chemical reaction between MIC and water raised the temperature to 400 degrees Fahrenheit (205 degrees Celsius) with a high-pressure build-up of **toxic** gases that were released.

2. chemical reaction creates heat and gases which increase pressure inside tank

3. safety valve releases gases into the atmosphere

MIC (Methyl isocyanate)

1. water enters tank

After hearing the alarms, terrified choking workers flee Bhopal's Union Carbide plant. (Artist's depiction)

17

The Challenger *space shuttle blasts skyward—but it is just moments from disaster. (Artist's depiction)*

external liquid fuel and propellant tank

orbiter

solid-fuel rocket boosters, SRBs

orbiter's three liquid-fuelled engines

USA

NASA Challenger

Space Shuttle Explosion

CHALLENGER, OFF FLORIDA, U.S.A., 1986

The five U.S. space shuttles were the only reusable spacecraft. Many times they launched into orbit, delivered satellites and space station supplies, and returned to Earth. However, just 73 seconds after launch on the 25th shuttle mission, *Challenger* was destroyed in an explosive fireball.

Each space shuttle had three main parts. The first was the white orbiter or space plane which went into orbit and returned to land safely on a runway. The second was a huge rounded external tank which supplied liquid fuel to the orbiter's three rocket engines during blast-off. The third part consisted of two solid-fuel boosters that also fired during a shuttle launch. The boosters and tank fell into the ocean as the orbiter continued into space. Most empty boosters were recovered and reused.

One booster was the cause of the *Challenger* disaster on January 28, 1986. After delays and unusually cold weather, the shuttle left the Kennedy Space Center at 11:38 a.m. All seemed well. Then smoke was seen coming from a joint between sections of the right-side booster. The joint was supposed to be sealed by strong rubber washers called O-rings, but they had failed. Jets of flame spurted from the gap at the liquid fuel tank. As the booster twisted around it broke the fuel tank and its two liquids, **propellant** and **oxidizer**, mixed and burned. Explosive flames engulfed the whole shuttle. The orbiter broke apart but the strongly-made crew cabin stayed mainly in one piece. It dropped like a stone for two minutes and 45 seconds and then hit the Atlantic Ocean. The crew, possibly still alive at that point, had no chance on impact. On March 9, the remains of the crew compartment and the astronauts' bodies were brought up from the sea bed.

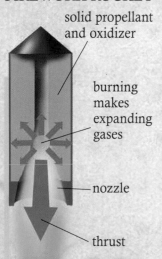

FIREWORK ROCKET

solid propellant and oxidizer

burning makes expanding gases

nozzle

thrust

THE SCIENCE OF ROCKETS AND FUELS

The two solid-fuel rocket boosters fired at take-off for two minutes and six seconds. Once alight, their cake-like fuel burned at a preset rate, with no way to turn it off—like a firework rocket. Hot, high-pressure gases from the burn rushed out the back, pushing the rocket forward. On the *Challenger* mission, cold had hardened the rubber O-rings between the booster sections. Also strong winds after lift-off twisted the booster and strained these joints. Hot gases and flames soon escaped through the gap.

SHUTTLE ROCKET BOOSTER

secure section joint

gap in section joint

Nuclear Accident

Unlike fires or floods, no one can see harmful radiation, or even feel it—until it gradually causes sickness, burns, and other deadly damage. This is what happened in the world's worst nuclear accident, on April 26, 1986.

The Chernobyl Nuclear Power Plant was in northeast Ukraine, near the border with Belarus. Four nuclear reactors produced over 4,000 megawatts of electricity, enough for one million homes. On that fateful day, engineers ran a test on Reactor Number 4. They turned off the high-pressure steam supply for the turbine generator to see if, as it gradually slowed down, it could still provide enough electricity to power pumps for the reactor's cooling water. This system could be used if the emergency diesel generators, which normally did the job, were faulty. But as the turbine ran down, the cooling water started to bubble and fizz. This decreased its cooling effect, the reactor warmed, its power output rose, the cooling water bubbled more, and so on. By accident, a young engineer pressed a button to insert all the reactor **control rods**. This caused an even bigger power surge. The core overheated, steam exploded out, then a second, bigger explosion happened, followed

THE SCIENCE OF NUCLEAR FISSION

All matter is made of tiny particles called atoms. At the center of each atom is its **nucleus** of even tinier particles. In certain substances, such as types of uranium, the nucleus slowly and naturally breaks apart, known as fission, to produce heat.

uncontrolled nuclear fission

controlled nuclear fission

REACTOR VESSEL

super-heated water out

control rods affect speed of fission

fuel rods produce heat

cool water in

reactor core

If purified amounts of these substances break up in an uncontrolled way, the result is a nuclear weapon (atomic bomb). Nuclear reactors keep fission under control in a reactor vessel to boil water into superheated water.

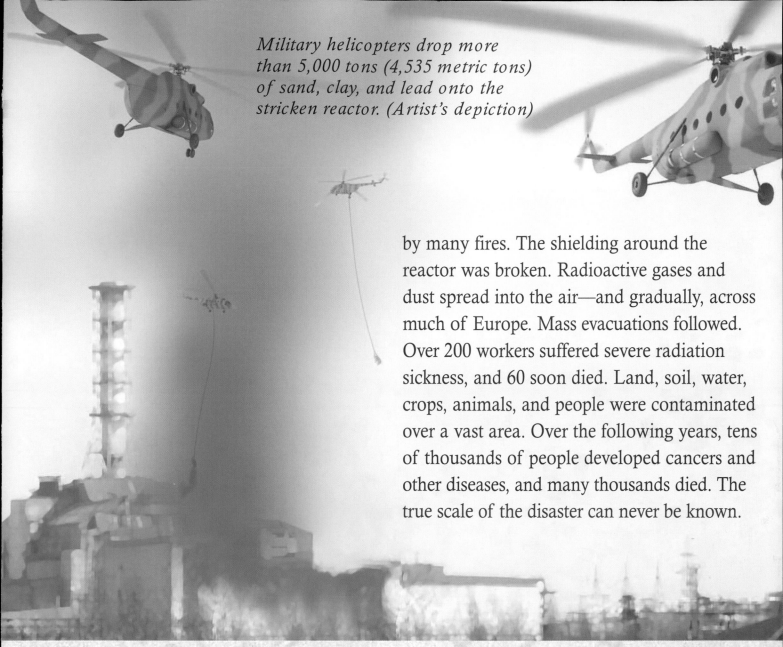

Military helicopters drop more than 5,000 tons (4,535 metric tons) of sand, clay, and lead onto the stricken reactor. (Artist's depiction)

by many fires. The shielding around the reactor was broken. Radioactive gases and dust spread into the air—and gradually, across much of Europe. Mass evacuations followed. Over 200 workers suffered severe radiation sickness, and 60 soon died. Land, soil, water, crops, animals, and people were contaminated over a vast area. Over the following years, tens of thousands of people developed cancers and other diseases, and many thousands died. The true scale of the disaster can never be known.

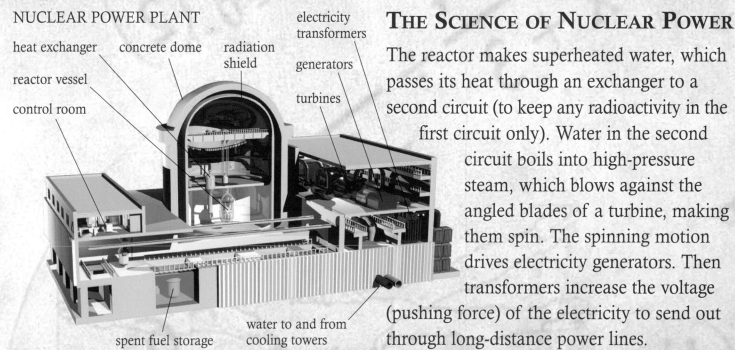

NUCLEAR POWER PLANT

heat exchanger   concrete dome   radiation shield

reactor vessel

control room

electricity transformers

generators

turbines

spent fuel storage

water to and from cooling towers

THE SCIENCE OF NUCLEAR POWER

The reactor makes superheated water, which passes its heat through an exchanger to a second circuit (to keep any radioactivity in the first circuit only). Water in the second circuit boils into high-pressure steam, which blows against the angled blades of a turbine, making them spin. The spinning motion drives electricity generators. Then transformers increase the voltage (pushing force) of the electricity to send out through long-distance power lines.

A second explosion rips through the torpedo room of the Russian submarine Kursk *as it crashes to the sea bed. (Artist's depiction)*

THE SCIENCE OF SUBMARINES

A sub has adjustable buoyancy. To rise, air is pumped into the ballast tanks and displaces water. The whole sub becomes lighter and ascends. Letting out the air makes it dive.

RISE   air pumped in

ballast tank

outer hull

water forced out

DIVE   air let out
water enters

Submarine Disaster

KURSK, BARENTS SEA, NORTH OF RUSSIA, 2000

Military submarines are the "Silent Service." They sneak around the world's oceans unseen, always ready for action. But in August 2000, the loss of Russia's *Kursk* brought submarines into the global news spotlight.

Kursk was a nuclear-powered submarine known as Oscar Class 2. It was 505 feet (154 meters) long, weighed over 15,000 tons (13,608 metric tons), had a crew of 112, and could possibly dive down 3,300 feet (1,000 meters). Weapons included 24 cruise missiles and many torpedoes.

On August 12, 2000, *Kursk* was taking part in a pretend battle with other Russian ships. In the torpedo room at the front, the crew loaded a dummy torpedo (without explosives) into Tube 4, ready to fire. But the torpedo was old and rusty. A powerful chemical inside, hydrogen peroxide, was used as an oxidizer to burn the kerosene fuel (since there is no oxygen gas under water). This powered a turbine to spin the torpedo's propellers. The hydrogen peroxide leaked out and reacted with the metals and rust to make high-pressure gases. These broke the kerosene tank and it burned with the oxidizer. The sudden explosion blew off the torpedo door, allowing water to flood in. The submarine, now nose-heavy, tipped forward and began to sink in the almost freezing water. As it hit the sea bed 355 feet (108 meters) down, a much bigger explosion smashed open more watertight compartments. This blast was caused by up to seven more torpedoes blowing up. Some crew survived in the sub's rear compartment, but as the power failed, they died from cold and lack of air. Their bodies and most of *Kursk* were finally raised the following year.

Like many ships, *Kursk* had watertight compartments inside. The first explosion allowed water into the front one and sent a blast wave into the next, injuring crew there. The second explosion damaged more compartments and was so powerful that scientific equipment hundreds of miles away showed it as a small earthquake. The extra-strong nuclear compartment resisted damage and the reactors automatically shut down safely.

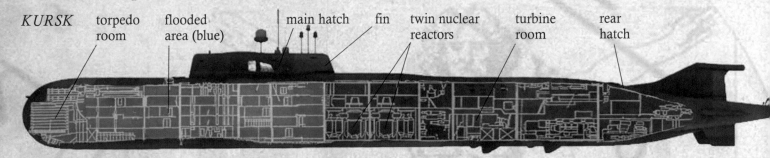

KURSK   torpedo room   flooded area (blue)   main hatch   fin   twin nuclear reactors   turbine room   rear hatch

Building Collapse

Every few years, a new skyscraper takes the record for the world's tallest building. The North Tower of the World Trade Center held the record from 1971 to 1973. In 2001 it, and its twin, were destroyed by terrorist attacks.

The World Trade Center's North Tower was 1,368 feet (417 meters) high, just six feet (two meters) taller than the South one. On an average weekday, each tower's 110 floors housed 25,000 workers and 100,000 visitors.

The al-Qaeda attacks took place on September 11, 2001 ("9/11"). The terrorists hijacked passenger jet planes. A Boeing 767 of American Airlines Flight 11 was flown into floors 93–99 of the North Tower at 8:46 a.m. Another Boeing 767 of United Airlines Flight 175 hit floors 77–84 of the South Tower soon after, at 9:03 a.m. Both planes from Boston were loaded with fuel, which ignited in several explosions and fires. Tens of thousands of people were trapped. The South Tower collapsed at 9:59 a.m., then the North Tower followed at 10:28 a.m. Each tower failed at its impact zone due to intense heat, especially weakening the joints between the floor deck frameworks and outer **perimeter** structure. It seems that as the floors broke, they pulled the perimeter inward. The top undamaged part of each tower fell almost straight down, crushing the lower part floor by floor. More than 2,750 people died, including plane crews, passengers, tower staff, visitors, firefighters, emergency workers, and ten hijackers.

THE SCIENCE OF SKYSCRAPERS

The two World Trade Center Towers had a design called the tube-frame structure. Much strength was in the four outer walls, each 208 feet (63 meters) long, with 59 steel columns, and narrow 18-inch (45-centimeter) glass panes between them. The central core of 47 steel columns and concrete reinforcing measured 135 by 87 feet (41 by 27 meters). The core housed the elevators, stairs, rest rooms, and services such as water, electricity, waste chutes, and air-conditioning.

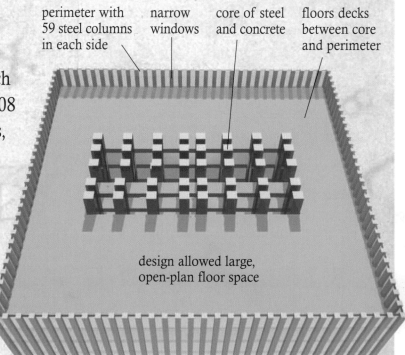

perimeter with 59 steel columns in each side

narrow windows

core of steel and concrete

floors decks between core and perimeter

design allowed large, open-plan floor space

The second hijacked airliner approaches the South Tower. (Artist's depiction)

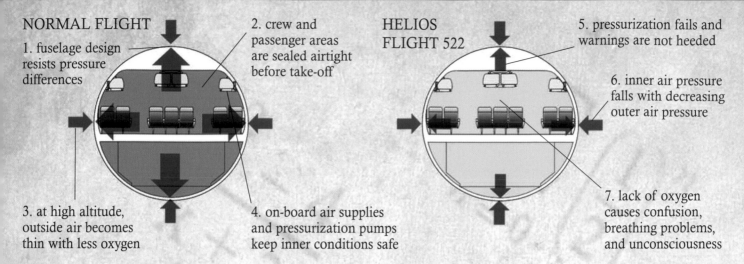

NORMAL FLIGHT

1. fuselage design resists pressure differences

2. crew and passenger areas are sealed airtight before take-off

3. at high altitude, outside air becomes thin with less oxygen

4. on-board air supplies and pressurization pumps keep inner conditions safe

HELIOS FLIGHT 522

5. pressurization fails and warnings are not heeded

6. inner air pressure falls with decreasing outer air pressure

7. lack of oxygen causes confusion, breathing problems, and unconsciousness

THE SCIENCE OF ATMOSPHERIC PRESSURE

Air pressure or atmospheric pressure is the pressing force in all directions on an object due to the weight of air above, extending to 60 miles (100 kilometers) above Earth's surface. With greater height or altitude, the air becomes thinner or lighter (less dense). This means it has less oxygen—the gas we must breathe in to stay alive. Large, high-flying planes like passenger jets have a cabin pressurization system. The air inside is kept at a comfortable pressure equal to an altitude of 5,000–7,000 feet (1,520–2,130 meters). With less pressure, less oxygen is available, leading to **hypoxia**. The body becomes breathless. The brain does not work properly, causing strange behavior, odd decisions, imaginary sensations, drowsiness, and loss of consciousness.

Two F-16 Falcon pilots try to work out what is happening to the Helios Flight 522 "ghost plane." (Artist's depiction)

Airliner Crash

For more than one hour, the Boeing 737 of Helios Airways Flight 522 circled in its holding pattern, waiting to land at Athens, Greece. But there was no one working the controls. Soon after, it ran out of fuel and crashed.

The Helios flight left Cyprus at 6:07 a.m. on August 14, 2005, with 115 passengers and six crew. This particular plane had been examined several times for pressurization and door problems. A ground engineer switched pressurization to "manual" to carry out a test, but did not reset it to "automatic." Apparently the crew did not notice this in their preflight and other checks. As the plane climbed, the air pressure inside fell, with less oxygen. Lack of oxygen causes the brain to do strange things, so the pilots did not realize what was happening. Their radio conversations with air traffic control and ground engineers became more confused. The cabin oxygen masks were released, but the pilots gradually lost consciousness. Two Greek Air Force F-16 fighter jets came near and saw one pilot's seat empty, with the other pilot slumped over. Autopilot took the plane into a holding pattern for landing. A cabin crew member tried to take control, but at that moment one engine ran out of fuel, then the other. At 12:04 p.m. the aircraft crashed into a mountain 25 miles (40 kilometers) from Athens. All 121 people on board died.

Without warning, the roadway deck of the I-35W bridge topples and falls during the evening rush hour. (Artist's depiction)

THE SCIENCE OF BRIDGES

Each bridge design is suited to a certain length, height above the valley, and types of rocks and supports at each end. A beam bridge may have midway supports. The truss bridge has a box-like shape, often with diagonal girders to form stress-resisting triangles.

truss bridge

beam bridge

Bridge Collapse

I-35W MISSISSIPPI RIVER BRIDGE, MINNEAPOLIS, U.S.A., 2007

The city's evening rush hour can be a frustrating crawl home along clogged roads. But any traffic jam is preferred to the disastrous failure of the I–35W Mississippi River Bridge in Minneapolis, on August 1, 2007.

All bridges are designed to strict guidelines so they can take loads such as heavy trucks and fierce winds, with strength to spare. In downtown Minneapolis, Minnesota, the eight-lane I–35W Mississippi River Bridge carried 140,000 vehicles daily on Interstate 35W. It was 1,907 feet (581 meters) long, with a truss-arch design. At 6:05 p.m. the central section suddenly collapsed, followed by parts on either side. With about 100 vehicles, it crashed down onto the river and banks below, causing 13 deaths and 145 injuries.

A detailed enquiry helped to explain the collapse. The bridge was full of slow traffic, but it was designed for that. However over the previous years, two extra lanes and more than two inches (five centimeters) of extra road surface had added much weight. Also on the bridge were more than 250 tons (227 metric tons) of construction vehicles and equipment, such as sand and water. This extra weight had strained parts called **gusset plates** used to join the steel girders. Just half an inch (12 millimeters) thick, they buckled with the increased load.

After a hectic but careful building program, the replacement I-35W Saint Anthony Falls Bridge opened in the same place—just over one year later, in September 2008.

An arch bridge's curve transmits forces around and down to the end supports. (The I–35W Mississippi River Bridge combined the truss and arch designs.) A cable-stayed bridge has tall towers or pylons with cables to the bridge and the bank, which pull with equal force in opposite directions. The suspension bridge's deck—the part with the walkway, roadway, railway, or both—hangs from two huge steel cables slung between pylons.

arch bridge

cable-stayed bridge

suspension bridge

Disasters World Map

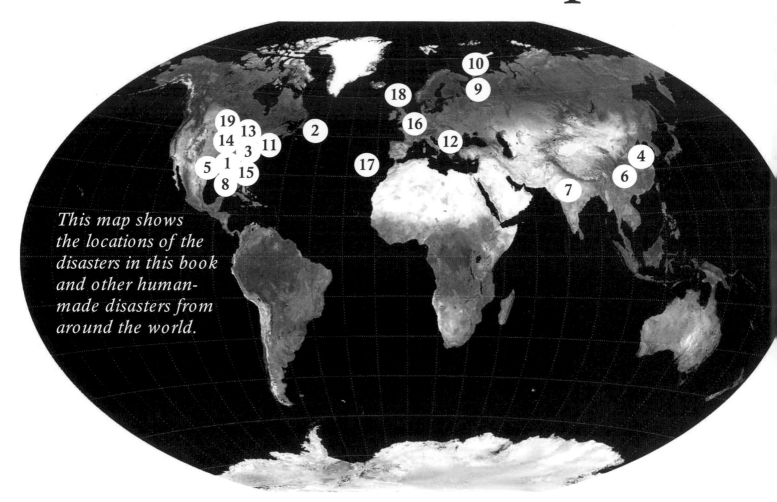

This map shows the locations of the disasters in this book and other human-made disasters from around the world.

1. South Pacific Railroad Yard Explosion, Texas, U.S.A., 1912

2. *Titanic* Sinking, Northwest Atlantic, 1912

3. *Hindenburg* Airship Fire, New Jersey, U.S.A., 1937

4. Benxihu Colliery Tragedy, Northeast China, 1942

5. Texas City Industrial Explosion, U.S.A., 1947

6. Banqiao Dam Failure, East-Central China, 1975

7. Bhopal Union Carbide Poison Gas Leak, India, 1984

8. *Challenger* Space Shuttle Explosion, off Florida, U.S.A., 1986

9. Chernobyl Reactor Nuclear Accident, Ukraine, 1986

10. *Kursk* Submarine Disaster, Barents Sea, 2000

11. World Trade Center Twin Towers Collapse, New York, U.S.A., 2001

12. Helios Airways Flight 522 Crash, Greece, 2005

13. I-35W Mississippi River Bridge Collapse, Minneapolis, U.S.A., 2007

14. Three Mile Island Nuclear Meltdown, Pennsylvania, U.S.A., 1979

15. *Columbia* Space Shuttle Re-Entry Disaster, over Texas, U.S.A., 2003

16. Modane Train Derailment, France, 1917

17. Tenerife Runway Airliner Collision, Canary Islands, 1977

18. Tay Railroad Bridge Collapse, Scotland, 1879

19. Great Chicago Fire, U.S.A., 1871

Glossary

buoyancy Whether an object is lighter or less dense than the fluid around it (such as air or water) and floats, or is heavier and sinks

carbaryl A chemical commonly used as an insect-killer, or insecticide, on farms and in parks, backyards, and gardens

control rods Rods pushed into the core of a nuclear reactor to absorb or soak up unwanted energy from nuclear fission

elevators On an aircraft, horizontal surfaces that move up or down, to control climbing or descending

flammable Able to ignite or catch fire easily

gusset plates Small sheets of strong material, usually metal, that join other pieces, such as long, thin girders

hypoxia Lack of oxygen in the body

nucleus The central part or middle part. The nucleus of an atom is its central part, made of particles called protons and neutrons.

oxidizer A substance that provides oxygen to allow burning or combustion, usually in a place lacking oxygen gas, such as under water or in space

perimeter The outer edge, border, or boundary of an area

propellant A substance that provides the force or thrust for movement, usually by burning or combustion

reciprocating Moving to and fro, or from side to side

rudders On an aircraft or ship, vertical surfaces that move from side to side, to control turning left or right

sluice gates Flaps or plates that open to allow a substance such as water to pass through a channel or pipe, and close to stop it

spontaneous combustion When something ignites or catches fire on its own, without an added spark or flame

static electricity Electrical charge that stays on an object, until it suddenly moves or discharges, often with a spark

toxic Harmful or damaging to living things

turbine A shaft or axle (long rod) with angled blades, like an electric fan. It spins around when high-pressure fluid, such as steam, air, or water, flows past the blades.

Index